IRAQ
IN FRAGMENTS

Based on the film by James Longley

LEVEL 3

SCHOLASTIC

Adapted by: Rod Smith
Publisher: Jacquie Bloese
Commissioning Editor: Helen Parker
Editor: May Corfield
Cover layout: Emily Briggs
Designer: Sylvia Tate
Picture research: Pupak Navabpour
Photo credits:
Page 6: Courtesy of the University of Texas Libraries, The University of Texas at Austin.
Pages 9, 29, 39 & 47: Daylight Factory/HBO Documentary Films/The Kobal Collection.
Pages 50 & 51: AFP; Bettmann/Corbis; Stockhaus.
Pages 52 & 53: D Greedy, J Readle, W Khuzle/Getty Images.
Pages 54 & 55: S Malkawi, S Hamed, M Di Lauro/Getty Images.
Pages 63: M Di Lauro/Getty Images.

Copyright © James Longley 2006. All Rights Reserved.

Published by Scholastic Ltd. 2009

No part of this publication may be reproduced in whole or in part, or stored in a retrieval system, or transmitted in any form or by any means, electronic, mechanical, photocopying, recording or otherwise, without written permission of the publisher. For information regarding permission write to:

Mary Glasgow Magazines (Scholastic Ltd.)
Euston House
24 Eversholt Street
London NW1 1DB

Fact File text and design copyright © Scholastic Ltd. 2009.
All rights reserved.

Printed in Singapore. Reprinted in 2010.

Contents

	Page
Iraq in Fragments	4–49
People and places	4
Introduction	7
Part 1 MOHAMMED OF BAGHDAD	8
Chapter 1: Remembering the city	8
Chapter 2: 'He loves me like his son'	12
Chapter 3: Back to school	16
Part 2 THE SHIAS GROW STRONG	22
Chapter 4: Moqtada al-Sadr and Sheikh Aws	22
Chapter 5: 'God is on our side'	27
Chapter 6: 'Who can believe America?'	31
Part 3 THE KURDISH SPRING	35
Chapter 7: Fathers and sons	35
Chapter 8: Hope and prayers	40
Chapter 9: A new vote	42
Chapter 10: Whose side is God on?	45
Epilogue	48
Fact Files	50–55
The country of Iraq	50
The invasion of Iraq	52
Sunnis, Shias and Kurds	54
Self-Study Activities	56–61
Glossary	62–63
New Words	inside back cover

PEOPLE AND PLACES

MOHAMMED is twelve years old. He lives with his grandmother in a Sunni area of Baghdad. He works in a garage, but his boss is often unkind to him.

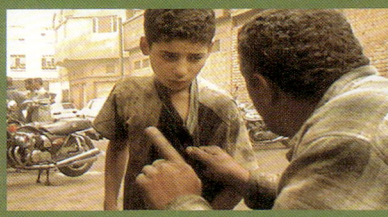

MOHAMMED'S BOSS is unhappy about life in Baghdad since the American occupation. He thinks the US attacked Iraq for its oil. He dislikes the new Iraqi government because he thinks it is unfair to Sunni people like himself.

MOQTADA AL-SADR is the religious leader of a special group of Shias. He thinks the US should leave Iraq and the country's people should follow the exact rules of Islam. His followers have their own newspaper and their own army.

SHEIKH AWS is the leader of Moqtada al-Sadr's followers in the city of Naseriyah. He is an intelligent man and a very good speaker.

SUNNIS AND SHIAS

Islam was founded by Mohammed in the seventh century AD. The Sunnis and Shias are both Islamic religious groups, but they believe in different things. Over the years, this has led to disagreements and fighting.

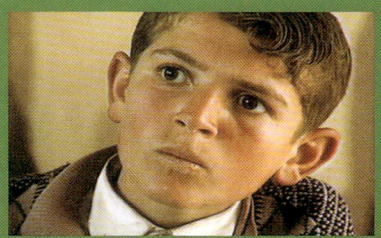

SULEIMAN is a Kurdish boy from Koretan, in northern Iraq. He wants to do well at school. This is difficult because his father is getting old and Suleiman has to look after the family's sheep.

MAHMOUD is Suleiman's father. He is happy that Saddam Hussein has gone. He hopes this will bring his people more power. He wanted Suleiman to study and work in the Islamic religion. He feels sad because this probably will never happen.

PLACES

NASERIYAH is Iraq's fourth largest city and an important centre for Moqtada al-Sadr's Shia followers. Sheikh Aws is their leader in the city.

KORETAN is a Kurdish village in the north of Iraq. The people here make a living from farming and making bricks.

BAGHDAD is the capital city of Iraq. It used to be beautiful but a lot of buildings were destroyed during the war. Both the new Iraqi government and the US Army have their main offices here.

Arbil
The capital city of the Kurdish area of Iraq.

Kirkuk
An important city in the Kurdish area. This city is the biggest producer of oil in Iraq.

Baghdad
The capital city of Iraq and the largest city in the country. About 6.5 million people live here.

Najaf
This city is the centre of Shia political power in the south of Iraq.

Naseriyah
The fourth largest city in Iraq. Another important centre for Shias.

Basra
Iraq's main port is here. This city also produces a lot of oil.

IRAQ
IN FRAGMENTS

Introduction

1st May 2003. It is the end of the war in Iraq. The Americans occupy Baghdad and Saddam Hussein has gone. Some people thought the change to democracy would follow smoothly. They were wrong. Saddam's rule was over, but the war between different groups of people inside the country was just starting.

Iraq's two main religious Islamic groups – the Sunnis and the Shias – were fighting because they wanted their own leaders to run the country. Then there were the Kurdish people in the north of the country. They didn't want to be part of Iraq at all and were fighting for their own state. Finally, there were the continued attacks on American soldiers. Many Iraqis didn't believe the reasons the United States gave for starting the war. Now it was over, they saw their soldiers as enemies and wanted them to leave as soon as possible. Iraq was a country in fragments.

American film director, James Longley, and his small team spent two years filming in different parts of Iraq. *Iraq in Fragments* is a story in three parts, and gives a picture of the lives of ordinary people touched by war. This is their story.

PART 1
MOHAMMED OF BAGHDAD

CHAPTER 1
Remembering the city

'I remember Baghdad before the war,' said Mohammed. He talked like an old man remembering his life, but he was only eleven. 'It was beautiful,' Mohammed continued. 'I remember the river. I remember the bridges. The river was full of fish. Now there's nothing. But then it was beautiful. It was so beautiful.'

We met Mohammed soon after we moved into the Sheikh Omar area of Baghdad. It is an area of small shops, cafés and garages. Although he was very young, Mohammed worked in one of the garages. He used to go to school, but now he worked instead. He told us he had no choice. His family needed the money.

'What about your father?' we asked.

'His name was Haithem,' Mohammed replied. 'But he

abandoned us.'

He told us that he now lived with his grandmother. They lived in the next street. Sometimes his mother and other relatives visited. But his grandmother was the one who looked after him.

The beautiful city Mohammed remembered wasn't beautiful any more. He had described it to us in the back of a car. We were sitting beside him. A man he worked with was driving us through the centre of Baghdad. We passed destroyed buildings and army checkpoints. Half a kilometre away, thick smoke was rising into the air. People hurried away from it. Was it from a bomb? We couldn't see. But we knew that these things were happening in Baghdad all the time.

We stopped at some traffic lights. An American soldier was standing at the side of the road with a gun in his hand. Nearby, some children were climbing over a pile of bricks. They stopped at the top and gave the soldier questioning looks. He looked back and made funny faces. He was trying to be friendly, but no one was laughing.

We drove on. In other parts of the city things seemed

almost normal. An Iraqi policeman stood in the middle of the road waving his hands at the traffic; people shopped in the markets; food-sellers cooked at the side of the road. But something was different. The fear was different. It was there with Saddam. But with Saddam, people knew what to expect. This was easier for the Sunnis than the Shias. Saddam was a Sunni and he hated the Shias. He hadn't allowed them to practise their religion freely. The parts of Baghdad where they lived had the worst time. For the Sunni areas, where Mohammed came from, life was easier. But then the war came.

Mohammed remembered it well. 'During the war it was so scary. Our house shook as the bombs fell. The war was above us. I was very afraid in the night. Then, one day, some people told us, "Baghdad has fallen. The Americans have taken the city." And now, they are still here. Their soldiers pass by. Their cars pass by. Their planes fly overhead. The world is so scary now.'

We arrived back at the garage. Mohammed's boss hardly noticed him return. He was sitting in the street with a group of men. They were playing a board game and talking angrily about the Americans. 'They only attacked us for the oil,' Mohammed's boss was saying. 'So why don't they take it and leave us alone? We don't care about the oil. Only the rich made money from it. We got nothing. For thirty-five years, Saddam took everything. The Americans will be even worse.'

'The Americans say they are not here for the oil,' said another man. 'That's what I read in the newspaper, anyway.'

A third man laughed. 'So why are they guarding Basra and Kirkuk? I'll tell you why. Because that's where the oil comes from.'

'And what about all the help they promised?' asked the second man. 'All the new jobs, food, and money.' He looked across at his friend. 'Have you had any yet?' he asked. Then he turned to Mohammed's boss. 'Have you?'

Both men shook their heads.

'Things are getting worse every day,' said the boss. 'Enjoy today, my friends, because tomorrow will be worse. If you don't believe me, look in the streets.'

'And George Bush* wants us to welcome him with flowers,' said the second man. 'Can you believe it?'

Mohammed stood in the garage doorway, listening. Suddenly, his boss turned and made a sign with his hand. The boss had an injury to his leg and couldn't move around easily. He didn't have to. Mohammed understood the sign. It was time for the boss's morning tea. Mohammed usually fetched it from a café in the next street. He picked up an empty glass and made his way there.

* George Bush was the President of the USA at the time of the Iraq war and occupation.

CHAPTER 2
'He loves me like his son'

On the way to the café, Mohammed described the area where he lived. 'The first thing that you see is the Abdul Khader Gaelani Mosque*. It is the highest building around here.'

We couldn't see it. The street was too narrow. There was only room for one car. Mohammed moved quickly, avoiding the traffic.

'I live opposite,' he said proudly when we reached the café. He waved his arm towards the other side of the street. 'If you ever want me, knock on the door and ask for Mohammed.'

Mohammed went into the café. We watched the café owner take his glass and fill it with tea. Mohammed thanked him and left, carrying the tea in one hand.

When we got back to the garage, Mohammed put the tea on a small table next to his boss. The boss said nothing as Mohammed gave him the tea. He just kept talking to his friends. Mohammed sat on the ground beside him.

Later, Mohammed told us about his boss. 'He tells me, "I am like your father",' Mohammed explained. 'It's true. He looks after me. He's nice to me. He loves me like his son. He doesn't hit me or call me rude names.'

Sometimes, we believed this was true. We often saw the boss pull Mohammed's nose in a friendly way. When he did that, they both laughed, and it seemed his boss was like a father. At other times, we weren't so sure.

ಌ ಌ ಌ

* A 'mosque' is a religious building where Muslims pray.

Later that day, Mohammed was playing a game in the street with one of his friends. The boss walked up and told the friend to go. Then he turned to Mohammed. 'Why aren't you cleaning the shop?' he asked angrily. 'You're always playing. Are we working here or playing? Why are you doing this?'

He pulled Mohammed's ear. This time it wasn't a joke. Mohammed ran into the shop. 'I've told you many times not to play,' the boss called after him. 'Some tools are missing. Why don't you look for them instead of playing?'

Mohammed sat in the doorway. He was looking at the ground and crying. The boss walked up and hit him on the head with a plastic pipe. Mohammed tried to cover his head as the boss called him rude names. 'Get up! Look at me!' the boss shouted. But Mohammed was too frightened to move.

ℭ ℭ ℭ

'We have to look at the world in a new way,' the boss's neighbour was saying, later that afternoon. The boss stood with his back to him, drinking water.

'We must forget the problems between Sunnis and Shias. We have to work together. We cannot allow the past to stop us moving forward.'

Mohammed was listening and trying to understand. After a few moments he went inside the shop. One of the boss's sons was counting banknotes. Mohammed sat beside him and helped.

'I never agreed with this occupation,' the boss said. 'Nobody got hurt except us, the poor. We will not get anything from it.' He walked into the shop, still speaking, 'The problems between Sunnis and Shias that you talk about are getting worse.'

Mohammed stood up as the boss came into the room. He tried to look busy and started cleaning. 'This new government is full of Shias. If you want a job you have to go to the Dawa Party*. They have to agree. And if you're Sunni, there's no chance of that.'

The boss's eldest son was sitting on the other side of the room. He was listening to his father but he wasn't saying anything. He had probably heard the same thing many times before.

Mohammed finished cleaning and walked over to the door.

'I wish Saddam were still here,' the boss said suddenly. 'OK, so he was hard on us. So what? He would never leave us in this position. No jobs, no security on the streets. He would never allow it.'

ଔ ଔ ଔ

After work, Mohammed went to meet his friends. They were sitting in a room at the end of the street watching a football game on TV. Mohammed joined them. But he

* The Dawa Party is a Shia political group.

wasn't really watching the football game. He was thinking about work: 'When I was younger, I used to wonder, "What is work? How do people work?" I knew nothing about it back then.'

In the past, Mohammed dreamt about the kind of work he wanted to do. The dreams continued even after he started working for his boss. He stopped going to school and got a job to earn money for his mother and grandmother. Then, after a time, he stopped dreaming about the perfect job.

ଔ ଔ ଔ

It was clear that Mohammed could see no other life but work. 'I'll keep on working,' he said. But his boss didn't agree. 'You must go back to school,' he told Mohammed. 'School will help you learn to read and write. This is very important. I don't want someone here who can't read or write. I will make you go. If you don't go, you will feel this.' He raised his hand. Mohammed stepped back. Once again he felt frightened.

CHAPTER 3
Back to school

The next day, Mohammed went back to school. We went with him but he was too excited to notice us much. Before the classes began, the head teacher talked to all the children in their play area outside. They stood in long lines with their hands by their sides, like soldiers.

'Welcome students,' the head teacher began. 'This year will not be like the others. There will be no cheating in school. The past is behind us. We have finished with unfair leaders and bad governments. You are the future of the new Iraq. If you do well at school, our country will be proud of you.'

Mohammed joined Class One – the lowest class. He had failed this class twice before. He was now four years older than the other students. This didn't seem to worry him. 'The important thing is to learn to read and write,' he said.

We sat at the back of the class and watched the first lesson. It was writing. The teacher was friendly and patient. She called the students up one by one. She watched as they wrote their names on the board.

Mohammed's turn came. He had forgotten how to write his name. But the teacher wasn't angry. She was very kind and helped him. Mohammed seemed to like the teacher and enjoy her lesson.

The second lesson was religion. The teacher started the lesson with a number of questions. 'Who is God?' he asked. 'And where is He?'

'In the sky,' one of the students said.

'Yes, that's right. And if we want to speak to God, what must we do?'

'Pray,' another student called out.

The teacher looked pleased with the answer. 'That is correct,' he said. 'And I will now teach you the prayer all Muslims use to address God. It is called the Opening Chapter. You must learn this, and never forget it.'

ଓ ଓ ଓ

Later, we asked Mohammed about his father, 'I can't remember him very well,' he told us. 'My father was a policeman. But he started saying bad things about Saddam so they put him in prison. I never saw him again.'

ଓ ଓ ଓ

That afternoon, Mohammed went to have his hair cut. There was a TV in the shop. Pictures of Saddam came on the screen. It showed Saddam after the Americans had caught him. Later, Mohammed told us about it. 'They were looking inside his mouth,' he said. 'They were searching his hair, his teeth, everything … And they showed pictures of him from before. He looked so proud back then.'

୪ ୪ ୪

Earlier that morning, the people in Mohammed's street had heard shooting. The garage boss was talking to his neighbour about it. 'Do you know what happened?' he asked.

The neighbour looked angry. 'It was a brother and a sister. The Americans asked them where they were going and told them to stop. The couple were frightened so they ran. The Americans killed them both. Can you imagine?' the neighbour shouted. 'A brother and sister!'

After this, everyone was very quiet. Mohammed sat in the doorway for a few minutes, then went to the main street. We followed.

In the main street, American soldiers were everywhere. They had guns in their hands and chewing gum in their mouths. Small crowds of Iraqis stood silently, watching.

'It's not safe here,' Mohammed said. 'There's no security. I want to escape and go abroad. I told my teacher I want to be a pilot. I want to fly a plane and see beautiful places. I often imagine that I'm high in the sky. I fly above the birds and look down. I see a beautiful place below me. This place is very different from Iraq. I fly down to the ground and think, "This is where I'll live".'

ര‍ ര‍ ര‍

The next day at school, Mohammed practised writing with his class. He listened to the teacher very carefully. His eyes followed her hands as she wrote on the board. When she repeated the words, Mohammed wrote the sounds in the air with his finger. He was working very hard now. Only one thing was on his mind. He wanted to make his dreams come true.

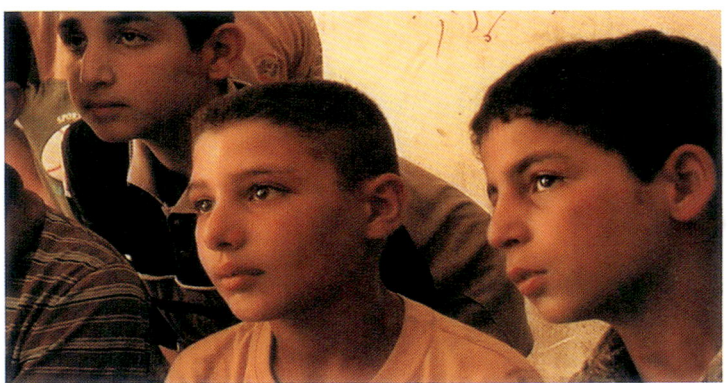

ര‍ ര‍ ര‍

The following morning brought bad news from the boss. 'Don't come to work any more from Tuesday,' he told Mohammed. 'Now you're at school you can only work an hour a day. That's no good to me. I'll find another boy to work for me instead.'

Mohammed felt bad. Although he earned less because of school, his family still needed the money. He knew they would be upset if he lost his job completely.

The boss saw that Mohammed was worried. 'Which do you prefer?' he asked. 'Work or school?'

'Work,' Mohammed answered quickly. It wasn't true but he didn't want to lose his job.

'OK,' he said. 'Write your name here, on this table.' Mohammed wrote his name.

'OK, and now your family name. Write it.'

'I only know my name,' Mohammed replied.

'You still don't know how to write your family name?' the boss shouted. He looked angry. 'When will you learn how to write "Haithem"? Next year? I don't know why you're in school. You learn nothing.'

Mohammed began to cry. He didn't want anyone to see so he covered his face with his arm and walked away.

'Why are you crying?' his boss called after him. 'Did I hit you? Come here! Look at me!'

Mohammed turned and walked back, looking frightened. The boss shook him. 'You dog! Bring a pencil tomorrow and write your father's name.' He pulled Mohammed's ear, hard.

The neighbour came out to see what was happening. He felt sorry for Mohammed and put an arm around his shoulder.

The boss looked up at his neighbour. 'He can't read or write after four years in school. It's better not to go. Come here!' he shouted to Mohammed. 'You're eleven years old and you still can't write. Go and tell your grandmother that you're leaving school. Now go away!'

ଓଃ ଓଃ ଓଃ

A few days later, Mohammed told us that he had found a new job. 'After my boss got angry with me I went home,' he explained. 'The next morning, my uncle came and I went with him to his shop. It's also a garage. But it's much bigger than my old boss's place. I started working with the men in my uncle's shop. They were nice. This new job is better for me. At my old job, the boss hit me and called me rude names. Here, no one does that. I will never go back to my old job. I would rather kill myself than go back there.'

We were happy that Mohammed had found a kinder person to work for. But we also hoped that he wouldn't forget about school and his dreams.

PART 2
THE SHIAS GROW STRONG

CHAPTER 4
Moqtada al-Sadr and Sheikh Aws

In the south of the country, the new Iraqi government feared one man more than any other. His name was Moqtada al-Sadr. He was the leader of a group of Shia fundamentalists*.

The al-Sadr family is famous in Iraq. Early in the twentieth century they helped to end British rule. Later, Moqtada's father refused to accept Saddam Hussein as Iraq's leader. He was killed on Saddam's orders.

After his father's death, Moqtada formed a Shia group that said religion must be part of politics. They started a newspaper called *al-Hawza*.

* 'Fundamentalists' follow the rules of their religion exactly.

The Shias had a hard time under Saddam. Then the Americans came and Saddam's rule ended. Suddenly, the Shias were free from the man they hated. But Moqtada wasn't grateful. He thought the Americans hadn't fought the war just to make life easier for his people. Like most Iraqis, he thought oil was the reason they had fought the war.

'America says they want to free Iraq,' Moqtada told his followers. 'That is a lie. They have just changed one bad government for another.'

The longer the Americans stayed, the angrier Moqtada and his group became. Other Shias were angry, too. They saw Moqtada as a strong voice against the occupation. More and more of them joined his group. It was now very strong in an area in the south of the country. But did everyone agree with Moqtada's ideas? We decided to go there and find out for ourselves.

ය ය ය

We went to Naseriyah, Iraq's fourth largest city. Here, the leader of Moqtada's group was a young man called

Sheikh Aws. The Sheikh was one of Moqtada's most intelligent followers. When he spoke, people listened.

The day we arrived, Sheikh Aws was addressing a large crowd. He was talking about his life under Saddam. 'I always loved religion,' he told his followers. 'When I was old enough, I entered the Hawza*. I saw Moqtada al-Sadr almost every day. He made me brave and I spoke against Saddam.'

We looked around at the crowd. Everyone sat very quiet, listening. 'They put me in prison for a full year,' Sheikh Aws went on. 'During that time I saw nobody. All I had was my religion. It was enough. And it's enough for every one of you. There is no fight between Sunnis and Shias. We are not enemies. Saddam made us enemies. Now he has gone and we must be free to celebrate religion in our own way.'

Sheikh Aws was a very good speaker. In his talk, he had spoken of the importance of practising religion freely. Saddam Hussein had not allowed Shias to do this. He had not allowed them to wear black or to sing and celebrate their religion in the street.

☙ ☙ ☙

The following morning, Sheikh Aws gave another talk. This time the subject was the Americans.

'They came to teach us Western democracy,' he told his followers. 'But what happens? They put us in prison. For what reason? They don't tell us. This is their democracy. But the only true democracy is Islam. They take away our oil and try to tell us how to think. Then, after all that, they say we are terrorists.

---

* The 'Hawza' is a religious training school.

'Where is the food and money they promised? They say they can't give it to us because of security problems.

But every day, huge trucks arrive with everything their soldiers need. How can anyone believe that the Americans care about the Iraqi people?'

୧୨ ୧୨ ୧୨

After the Sheikh's talk, we drove with him and some of his men to a meeting. It was in a large hall just outside Naseriyah. On the way, the Sheikh spoke about their plan to free Iraq. 'We must hold elections in our own areas,' he told us. 'National elections will happen after July. But we must act before then. The United States wants to be sure that national elections will produce a good result for them. So they have put their Iraqi friends in local government. When national elections come these people will vote for an Iraqi government. But it will not be a government of the true Iraqi people. It will be a government friendly to America. We have to stop that. So we will hold local elections here in Naseriyah and all our cities. Then the people we choose will order these "friends" of America to go. After this, national elections will produce a truly democratic Iraqi government. The Americans may not accept this. But then the world will see the lie of their "democracy."'

The first speaker at the meeting talked of possible problems. 'The Americans may try to stop us holding these elections,' he said. 'But they will find out that the Shias are Islam's strongest fighters. Our people will fight in peaceful ways. They will refuse to accept the orders of our enemies. They will lie down in front of US tanks in the street. They will show the world we cannot be used like dogs. But right now, the most important thing is to prepare ourselves.'

Everyone agreed.

CHAPTER 5
'God is on our side'

As the parties were preparing for the elections, news came of a problem in the local market. 'People are selling alcohol there,' someone reported.

Islamic law does not allow people to drink or sell alcohol. But Moqtada's group had no power in local government. The local government was friendly to America. They would do nothing to stop the alcohol sellers. This would not change until after the new elections. Moqtada's group couldn't wait that long. Their leaders were angry. Selling alcohol was against God's law. If necessary, they would act alone.

Sheikh Aws addressed his followers in Naseriyah's main square. 'People are bringing the dangers of alcohol into our market,' he said. 'Men and women pass by and say nothing. The government does nothing. We cannot stay silent. This is an Islamic city! God is telling us to show these people what is right. We are telling them now: "You have three days to stop these activities." After three days, the Mehdi Army* will go into the market. If these people are still there, they will take them away. The enemies of our religion cannot win. God is on our side.'

After Sheikh Aws' talk, there were celebrations. A young boy sang a religious song and the men moved slowly, hitting their chests**. At the edge of the crowd, the soldiers of Islam were getting ready.

ଔ ଔ ଔ

Three days later, the Mehdi Army went into the market. They sat in the back of open trucks. They carried machine guns and their faces were covered.

The trucks stopped and the Shia soldiers jumped out. They fired their guns in the air. People screamed and ran away. The soldiers moved among the frightened crowd. They kicked over tables and took away any alcohol they found.

Some soldiers held the people they thought were alcohol sellers. Others hit them with sticks. Then the soldiers threw them into the back of the trucks.

After a few minutes the whole market was empty. The trucks drove away. The prisoners sat in the back looking hurt and frightened.

The soldiers took them to a large house in Naseriyah.

* The 'Mehdi Army' are Moqtada al-Sadr's soldiers.

** Shias hit their chests to remember their religious leaders from the past: Imam Ali and Imam Hussein.

Many of the prisoners said they were not alcohol sellers at all. 'We weren't doing anything,' one man screamed. 'We were only passing by.'

'Just keep quiet!' shouted one of the soldiers.

The prisoners took no notice. 'How can we be alcohol sellers?' one of them asked. 'Alcohol sellers would run. We didn't run. We saw people selling alcohol. They went when you came. You took us instead and let them go free.'

There were problems outside the house, too. That evening a woman with a small child stood in the street in front of the house. She was talking angrily to one of the Mehdi Army soldiers. Her husband was a prisoner inside the house. 'You've made a mistake,' she said. 'My husband was selling car parts, not alcohol. Just let me talk to him.'

'If he did nothing wrong, we'll let him go,' the soldier replied. 'We need to talk to him first. You can't see him until we've finished.'

'My God!' the woman said. 'A man has problems earning enough money for his family and you make him a prisoner. What can we do? This morning we didn't even eat any breakfast.'

Inside the house, the noise continued. 'I thought we were saved from Saddam,' one of the prisoners shouted. 'Now you tie our hands and cover our eyes as he did. How can this happen, brother?'

'Stop your noise!' the soldiers' leader shouted.

But the prisoner wouldn't be quiet. 'Even God cannot accept this,' he said.

ଓ ଓ ଓ

In the end, the Mehdi Army freed all the prisoners. Had they acted too quickly and made mistakes? No one could be sure. But their message was clear. They would not allow alcohol into their city.

'We are living in dangerous times,' Sheikh Aws told us later. 'The Americans attack our religion. They bring their bad ways of living into our city. They will do anything to destroy us. They fear the Mehdi Army will drive them from Iraq. But soon, there will be elections. We are choosing a peaceful way to change our future. But if this doesn't work, God will show us another way to end this occupation.'

CHAPTER 6
'Who can believe America?'

Many Shias soon believed 'another way' was necessary. This followed the arrest of one of Moqtada's assistants. His name was Mustapha Yacoubi. The police wanted to question Yacoubi about the murder of another Shia leader, Sayed al-Khoei. They described al-Khoei as an enemy of Moqtada. They said Moqtada had told Yacoubi to arrange the murder of al-Khoei. Because of this, they also wanted to arrest Moqtada.

'This is just an excuse,' Moqtada told his followers. He knew he was making the Americans nervous. They wanted the police to put him in prison. It would be one less problem for them. He called the reasons for the arrest 'lies'.

In the end, it made no difference. The police arrested Yacoubi and closed the *al-Hawza* newspaper. This made the Shias very angry.

One afternoon, a large number of them went on a demonstration to a place just outside the city of Najaf. At the time Spain had many soldiers in this area. The demonstration went terribly wrong. The date was 4th April 2004.

One man described what happened. 'We came out for a peaceful demonstration. We were asking the government to let Mustapha Yacoubi out of prison. Many people came. The demonstration stopped in front of the police. Behind them, there were Spanish soldiers. They were standing with their guns ready to shoot. People were angry and they pushed the police back. The police fired their guns in the air. Some people in the demonstration also had guns.

A fight started and many people were shot.'

The shooting lasted for three hours. Twenty people were killed. Four of these were occupation soldiers. More than two hundred demonstrators had terrible injuries. Blood poured into the sand as people carried them to the nearest hospital. 'Is this democracy?' cried one man as they carried him away.

ଔ ଔ ଔ

There was also trouble in Baghdad. There, seven American soldiers died in fights with Moqtada's Mehdi Army. This followed news of the torture of Iraqi prisoners by guards at the Abu Ghraib prison. Iraqis were very angry about this.

The USA tried to calm the Iraqi people. 'No American can accept these terrible acts,' said US president George Bush on TV. 'We will find out what happened. If anyone ordered the torture of prisoners, we will arrest them. The whole world will find out the truth.'

Sheikh Aws didn't believe that this would happen. 'Who can believe America?' he asked. 'Can any Muslim believe that they want to help us? God is with those who fight these lies. And death to any American spies among us. You saw what happened in Baghdad. They were hanged in the street. The same will happen to anyone who gives information to the Americans.'

In Najaf, Moqtada was also asking his followers to fight. 'If Vietnam can win a war against America, then so can we,' he said.

Soon the streets of Najaf, Naseriyah and other Shia cities of the south were filled with Moqtada's men. They carried his picture and shouted his name. Traffic stopped and people stood at the side of the road, watching.

Not everyone wanted to join Moqtada's fight. 'If Moqtada and his people take power, ' said one man, watching Moqtada's crowds, 'it will be like the return of Saddam. Look around this city. It is empty. It's like a ghost town. Moqtada's men rule. People are frightened. They stay in their homes. They think it's safer. Maybe, but it's no way to live.'

ଔ ଔ ଔ

The next day, some of the excitement had passed. The city of Najaf was calmer and ordinary Iraqis were giving their opinions about the occupation.

'America promised one thing, but they did something else,' said one man. He was sitting outside a café with his friends. 'They said they came to free us, but then they became occupiers. They said they came to help us. But then they turned against us. That is America. You can't believe anything they say.'

'You know what America's biggest problem is?' said his friend. 'They think guns are the answer to everything. They bring in their armies and think the war is won.

This won't work. You have to study the Iraqi people if you want to know them. You have to learn their history and the way they do things. Without this, success is impossible.'

As he spoke, shooting sounded from the centre of the city. Outside a mosque, relatives were crying. They were crying for dead husbands, brothers and sons.

'There is only one God,' shouted the crowds. 'And America is the enemy of God!'

ೞ ೞ ೞ

As hate for the occupation grew, one thing was becoming clear. The whole area was now too dangerous for Westerners. Later that day, we left Najaf. We got on a train and looked back at the troubled city. Slowly, it disappeared from view. We wondered if we would ever see it again. But not for long. Our thoughts were now on another place – a place far beyond Baghdad.

It was time to head north.

PART 3
THE KURDISH SPRING

CHAPTER 7
Fathers and sons

Northern Iraq is like a different country. The dangerous roads north of Baghdad slowly disappear. There are fewer checkpoints. You enter a land of soft hills and yellow wheat. The people here are Kurds, not Arabs. This part of Iraq is called Kurdistan. For more than a hundred years the Kurds have wanted to make it their own national state. Saddam Hussein was afraid of this. So he made a lot of Arabs move here to live. He also used any excuse to attack Kurdish towns and villages. Many Kurds died under Saddam's rule. They are probably happier than anyone that he has gone. Most of the Arabs that had to move here have also gone.

Still further north, clouds of black smoke rise from strange buildings on the tops of some of the hills. These are ovens for making bricks. The smoke comes from the oil fires used to make the bricks. In the middle of this area there is a little village called Koretan. After the dangers of the south, it is a peaceful place.

With Saddam gone, people were optimistic. Elections would take place soon. The elections were for a new Iraqi government. The Kurds hoped that they would be able to elect their own people. If that happened, it might help them to form their own state one day.

What would happen? We moved to Koretan to find out.

The people of Koretan live a simple life. They earn money from making bricks, growing wheat, fruit and vegetables, and keeping sheep. We made friends with two local farmers. They were neighbours and the two families were very close. The fathers and sons were best friends and spent a lot of time together. After six months, they hardly noticed we were there and filming them became easier.

In Koretan, it seemed that the land changed more than the people. During the summer, it is very hot and dry and the ground is burnt yellow by the sun. In winter, it is cold. Sometimes it snows. In spring, the hills turn pale green with new grass. Autumn is the most exciting season. This is when the hills are alive with fire and smoke.

We filmed a conversation about the changing seasons. Bizhar, one of the sons, was remembering the past year like a set of pictures.

'I remember all the days,' he said. 'They pass before my eyes. In autumn, they work the brick ovens. I go there with my friends. We sit and watch the fires for hours.'

In summer, the late afternoon is a hot, dead time of day. This is when Bizhar's father often played a board game with his neighbour, Mahmoud. They used different size stones on a board of black and white squares.

'You will lose,' we heard Bizhar's father tell Mahmoud one afternoon.

'No, you will lose,' Mahmoud replied. He was an older man and spoke to his neighbour like a father to a son.

'It's not fair,' said his friend a few minutes later. 'You take back your moves. That's cheating. When you do that, I don't want to play any more.'

Mahmoud smiled. 'You always say that when you lose,' he replied.

His friend smiled back. 'OK, you've won,' he said. 'But it wasn't easy.'

The two men often pretended to be angry. But they weren't serious. It was just a game.

ଔ ଔ ଔ

Later, Mahmoud talked about his life. 'My father named me Mahmoud. It was the name of a religious leader. He wanted me to do well so he sent me to school. But a short time after that, he died. Then the rest of the family wanted me to leave school and work. "Look after the sheep," they said. "You don't know how to study. You will never get anywhere through studying." So I had to leave school and look after the sheep. I don't want that to happen to my son. I want him to be different.'

Mahmoud's son was called Suleiman. He was Bizhar's best friend. Bizhar called him Sulei. 'We are like brothers,' Bizhar explained. 'And as we get older, we will stay good friends. We have always been very close. We play together all the time. It's the same at school. We walk there together every day. If anyone attacks Sulei, I will fight them. He does the same for me.'

For Bizhar and Suleiman, school offered a chance to escape life as a poor farmer. But Suleiman was more serious about it. He worked very hard at school and often talked about finding a good job in the future. But he also knew it wouldn't be easy. 'You have to study as much as possible,' Suleiman told us, 'It's not enough. It is always too little. If you spend all your time studying, maybe you'll become a doctor or something. If you don't study at all, you'll have to take any job you can find. At the moment, I hope I can do well enough just to pass my exams.'

Suleiman's class teacher was happy with his work. She often used Suleiman's sentences as an example in her English classes.

The same was not true of the head teacher. 'He is always telling me that I will fail,' said Suleiman. 'But who knows about the future? I think he says things like that just to make me study more.'

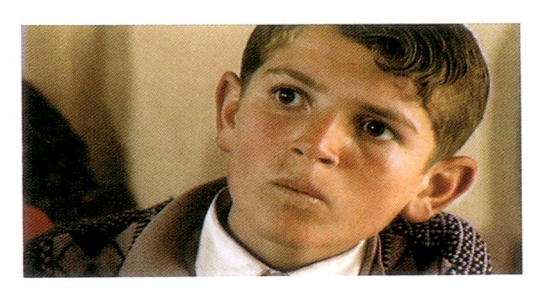

This could be true. After school, Suleiman doesn't have much time to study. His father is growing old and he has to help look after the sheep with his brother, Rosho.

'I'm always with the sheep,' said Suleiman. 'Winter and summer, it's always the same. But I don't want to leave school. I want to go to college and get a good job.'

CHAPTER 8
Hopes and prayers

Outside Bizhar and Suleiman's lives, serious things were happening. The Kurds and Arabs of Iraq had never been friends. During and after the war against Saddam this dislike grew. Now they were complete enemies. The Arabs said that the Kurds had brought America to Iraq. The occupation was their fault. They attacked them for not being true believers in Islam. The Kurds were just as angry towards the Arabs.

'The Iraqi Arabs want to kill us all,' said Mahmoud one evening. He was talking with his friends around the brick ovens. Their faces shone red in the light of the fire. 'They say we are not true believers. But what is a believer for them? Someone who will kill himself to attack America? They are crazy. This is not true religion. The Koran doesn't say this. It says that any place touched by the light of the sun will be ruled by Islam. Killing yourself does not bring light. If there is any true religion left, it is among our people, the Kurds.'

For Bizhar's father, there was nothing wrong in celebrating the end of Saddam Hussein. 'He destroyed our villages,' he said. 'He tried to change our land into an Arab area. We couldn't accept this. We fought. Too many lives were lost. Now we can never become friends. It is too late for that.'

Most people in Koretan were grateful for the occupation. 'God brought America to the Kurds,' another man explained. 'They made Iraq free and we came from darkness into the light. In the south, the fighting continues. But there's been enough war in Iraq. I say it is time that everyone puts down their guns and practises politics instead.'

'We hope political elections will bring us our own government,' Mahmoud told us later. 'Compare us to the Jewish people. They have their own state and their own government. They are strong and free. Why can't we be the same? I may not live to see the birth of a new Kurdistan. But I hope my children will see it.'

ଔ ଔ ଔ

Later, Mahmoud spoke to us about the rest of his life and Suleiman's future. 'I will die soon,' he said. 'For the rest of my life I will spend most of my time in the mosque, praying to God. I wanted Suleiman's life to be spent in religion. I told myself, "I have six sons. Five can be for this life, but let one of them be for God." But this hasn't happened. I wanted Suleiman to be different. I still pray it will happen.'

CHAPTER 9
A new vote

In Islam, Friday is the most important day of the week. Every Friday, all true believers go to the mosque to pray and listen to the Imam*. When we went, the subject of the Imam's talk was the elections.

'We ask God to hear our prayers on this Friday,' the Imam said. 'The elections will be soon. Everyone must vote. It is very important for our future, our people, and our country. There must be no work on election day. We must give this one day to save our unhappy nation. For years we have fought in the mountains. We have fought the Arabs and all those who occupy our land. But this vote is more important than a hundred bombs. So go, my people, and change the history of our nation.'

ఠ ఠ ఠ

Election day came. The peace of Koretan disappeared as people tried to push their way into the election hall. We realised then how thin this peace really was. Many people didn't like the present Kurdish leaders.

'Our leaders have grown fat,' one old man told us, 'while we poor people go hungry.'

Another man agreed. 'These people want us to vote for them. They smile and make false promises. But they will take our votes today and give nothing back tomorrow. I will not vote for these people. They only want to fill their pockets. I will only vote for those who I know will help the poor.'

* An 'Imam' is an Islamic religious leader.

Although there were disagreements, there was general excitement about one thing. Everyone felt that the voice of Kurdistan would be heard for the first time. 'Until now the world has not known who we are,' one man told us. 'With these elections, that will change.'

'Kurdistan! Kurdistan!' the people shouted.

Managing the election wasn't easy. The people weren't used to voting. Many of them crowded round the doors of the election hall and refused to stand in line. The soldiers guarding the building got angry. 'You can't stand there,' one of them shouted at a group of people. 'Move away!' He pushed them roughly. We were worried that a fight might start.

Luckily, an election officer came out of the hall and stopped things going too far. 'Let them come in, brother,' she said to the soldier. She turned to the people waiting to get in. 'Please be patient,' she said.

Inside the hall was just as noisy as outside. It was full of people wondering what to do. Some looked excited, others looked lost. But in the end, everyone got the chance to vote – even those who couldn't read or write.

Back outside the hall, an old man had just voted. He wasn't optimistic for the future of Iraq. 'It will be hard for Kurds, Sunnis and Shias to live together,' he told us. 'The future of Iraq will be in three pieces.'

'Iraq is not something you can cut into pieces,' a young girl said. 'It is a country. How can you cut a country into pieces? With a knife?'

ಌ ಌ ಌ

Later that day we found Suleiman out in the fields with his sheep. He too was filled with the excitement of election day. 'Kurdistan is beautiful,' he said. 'We must protect it like our own eyes. We must not let our enemies occupy our land. With God's help, we will succeed. God will make us strong.'

After these words, he went quiet. We looked at the sheep standing in the fields. The sun was going down and the light was golden. For a few moments, peace had returned.

CHAPTER 10
Whose side is God on?

Winter arrived soon after the elections. One morning, there was snow on the ground. It wasn't very deep, but Bizhar, Suleiman and their friends made snowballs and threw them at their friends. Everyone was soon running around, laughing. For the first time, we were seeing a fight that wasn't real. The snow didn't last long. Winter is a very short season. Soon, spring arrived. The earth turned pale green and the days grew warmer.

'I thank God when spring arrives,' Bizhar said to us one day. 'I had forgotten how beautiful it was. I forget many things. They just don't stay in my mind. When I talk of the beautiful things I remember, people tell me I'm dreaming.' He looked around at the fresh, green fields. 'How can this be a dream? I've never seen such a dream.'

Bizhar was happy. But Suleiman wasn't. We saw them later, walking home from school together. Suleiman looked sad.

We soon found out why. He told us that he had to leave school. At first, we couldn't believe it. His plans for the future had seemed so real. How could he abandon them so quickly?

But he hadn't abandoned them. He had no choice. He explained, 'My family told me, "You must look after the sheep and work in the brick ovens." Father is too old and weak. He can't work any more. And without work, there is no money.' Suleiman looked at Bizhar, smiled sadly and turned to us. 'They are right. For now, I must forget the future. I have no right to go to school. My father spent his life looking after me. Now I must look after him. That is my job now. I am the only one left of the family who can work.'

We saw the brick ovens ahead of us. Suleiman ran forward and picked up one of the bricks. He held it up in the air. 'They won't let anyone work here if they are not a good brick cutter,' he said. 'A lot of strong-looking guys come looking for work. But no one gives them any. They don't have the skills. So they go home and lie around all day. That won't happen to me. I am lucky. At least I have a job. In the day, I will work at the brick ovens and then look after the sheep. I am building a life.' He turned to Bizhar. 'Isn't that right?'

Bizhar didn't answer. Suleiman was really telling himself he was doing the right thing. We wondered if he really believed it.

෴ ෴ ෴

When he arrived home, Suleiman washed his face, hands and feet outside the house. Then he got down on his knees and prayed.

Inside, his father was talking to a young man about the occupation of Iraq. 'Now the war is over,' Mahmoud was saying. 'Today, everything in Iraq is managed by America. No one can escape the hand of America.'

Through a window behind Mahmoud we could see a group of children around a fire. One of them was Suleiman. As the fire grew stronger they started dancing around it.

Mahmoud lit a cigarette and turned to the younger man. 'Two men are about to fight,' he said. 'They are both big and strong. Then someone asks them, "Whose side is God on?" They look at this person and one of them answers, "God is always on the side of the winner. Whoever wins, God is on his side."'

What about Suleiman? Was God on his side, too? Would he go back to school and escape the life of a poor farmer?

We heard him walking back towards the house with his friends. When he reached the front door, he called out, 'I'm going. God be with you.'

ര‍ ര‍ ര‍

Several months later we left Iraq, knowing that these people still had their lives to live. What would happen to them all? Iraq is a broken country in many ways, and its future is in the hands of the Iraqi people. We hope *Iraq in Fragments* will help others to understand better this troubled country and its people.

EPILOGUE

The film *Iraq in Fragments* came out in early 2006. It described a broken country. But it also showed many Iraqi people acting together to make their country whole again. Were they successful? Is Baghdad still a frightening place for young boys like Mohammed? Is Shia leader Moqtada al-Sadr still asking his followers to fight the American occupation? And are the Kurds and Arabs of the north still enemies?

There is no simple answer to these questions. In 2007, the Americans sent more soldiers to Iraq and Baghdad became a little safer. Then, Moqtada al-Sadr agreed to stop fighting until a new Iraqi government was formed: he wanted to find out how much power his Shia people could win. And the Kurds now have their own government with more power for their areas in the north of the country. America has also agreed to move its soldiers out of Iraq's main cities by June 2009. They are planning to leave the country completely by 2011.

This more peaceful time has lasted almost two years, but there are signs that things are becoming worse again. Moqtada and his followers want the Americans to leave Iraq now. On 21st November 2008 they burnt a large picture of George Bush in the centre of Baghdad. In that same month, thirteen US soldiers were also killed.

The Kurdish people of the north have been the most successful group in Iraq. But now they have problems, too. They still see Iraqi Arabs as their enemies and both groups are fighting over the oil-rich city of Kirkuk. Will the local Kurdish government have power over the city? Or will that power belong to the central Iraqi government? No one knows. But the disagreement is not helping the country join together.

A difficult road lies ahead before Iraq can become a 'whole' country again. We, in the rest of the world, can help. We can only do this by understanding the Iraqi people and their problems. There is no better first step than listening to their voices in *Iraq in Fragments*.

FACT FILE

The Country of Iraq

For many people, Iraq is a country at war; a dangerous place, without laws. But it is also a beautiful country, rich in history and natural beauty.

WHERE IS IRAQ?

Iraq is in the Middle East. It lies between Saudi Arabia and Iran at the top of the Persian Gulf. It is about the same size as California in the USA.

What is it like?

Iraq is mostly desert, but there are mountains in the north and a short coastline in the south. Farming land lies between its two rivers, the Tigris and the Euphrates. Iraq is hot in the summer and cool in the winter. It is a country rich in oil.

IRAQ IN MODERN TIMES

The British occupation of Iraq ended in 1947. Different Arab kings ruled the country until 1958, when the military took power. Then, in 1968, the Baath Socialist Party came to power. In 1979, Saddam Hussein became their leader. He made himself President of Iraq, and the country entered dangerous and troubled times.

Saddam Hussein

Saddam killed other people who wanted to be President. Anyone who didn't agree with him was killed or sent to prison. Saddam was a Sunni. He hated the Shias. He thought that Iran – a Shia country – would help the Shias in Iraq take power. So, in 1980, he started the Iran-Iraq War. The war ended in 1988. But two years later, Saddam invaded Kuwait. The United Nations (UN) agreed to a military

HISTORY OF IRAQ

The area now called Iraq was once known as Mesopotamia, the home of the Sumerians. Dating from 5000 BC, these people formed the world's first-known civilization. They produced the earliest form of writing.

They were followed by the Babylonians, whose name came from their capital city, Babylon. This city was famous for its hanging gardens.

The Hanging Gardens of Babylon

They were built by King Nebuchadnezzar II and were one of the 'Seven Wonders of the World'. The area became the centre of the Islamic Empire. In 762, Baghdad became its capital. Later, the Ottoman Turks ruled Iraq until the British took the area in 1917 during the First World War.

What do you know about your country's history? Talk about it in class.

Saddam Hussein celebrating his birthday

The UN had ordered sanctions to stop Iraq producing dangerous weapons. The Americans said the sanctions weren't working. Finally, in 2003, they used this as a reason to invade Iraq and destroy Saddam.

attack to free the country. This was the First Gulf War.

What do these words mean? You can use a dictionary.
invade / invasion   military   sanctions   weapons   civilization   empire

FACT FILE

THE INVASION

In March 2003, the American army and their allies invaded Iraq. The war in Iraq and the following occupation has been a subject of heated discussion for many years since. Here, we look at the facts behind the invasion.

WHAT WERE THE REASONS FOR THE INVASION?

Saddam Hussein

George Bush

Saddam Hussein was still Iraq's leader after the First Gulf War. The United Nations (the UN) had ordered sanctions to stop Iraq producing dangerous weapons. However, the Americans said that the sanctions weren't working and that Saddam still had chemical weapons. When George Bush became the President of the United States in 2000, his government decided that Saddam must go.

The government of the USA knew that world opinion would be against invading Iraq without a good reason. The attack on the World Trade Centre in New York in 2001 gave them that reason.

They said that Saddam had helped the attackers, and that he was making chemical weapons. The US then gave a third reason for an invasion: to free the Iraqi people from Saddam. They hoped these reasons would persuade the UN to agree to an invasion.

> The United Nations was formed at the end of the Second World War. It is made up of nearly 200 countries. It tries to protect people around the world, and stop wars.

> **What do these words mean? You can use a dictionary.**
> invade / invasion   ally
> chemical weapon   persuade
> inspector

OF IRAQ

DID THE UN AGREE WITH THE INVASION?
No. The UN said that there were no signs that Saddam was hiding weapons. Iraq had allowed weapons inspectors inside the country. They wanted them to have more time to search, but the USA and its ally, Britain, decided to invade anyway.

WAS THE INVASION POPULAR?
No. News of the invasion plan produced the biggest demonstrations against war in history.

Millions of people wanted to show that they disagreed with the invasion. Many people said that the Americans wanted to invade Iraq for its oil. It made no difference. The USA gave Saddam 48 hours to leave Iraq, but he didn't go.

An anti-war demonstration

What are your thoughts on the invasion of Iraq?
Talk about it in class.

HOW LONG DID THE FIGHT LAST?
The invasion started on 20th March 2003. The US and its allies were too strong for the Iraqi military.

On 1st May 2003 George Bush said the war was over. However, since then, more than four thousand American soldiers have been killed. By 2006, Iraq was described as 'the most dangerous place on earth'.

WHAT IS THE POSITION IN IRAQ TODAY?
In 2007, the USA decided to send in more soldiers. They wanted them to protect the Iraqi people, and to help and train Iraqi soldiers. Today, Iraq is becoming safer, but it is still too early to say that its problems are over.

FACT FILE

SUNNIS, SHIAS

In Iraq, there are two main Islamic groups, the Sunnis and the Shias. What are the differences between them, and who are the Kurds?

THE SUNNIS: PEOPLE OF THE PROPHET

Most of the world's Muslims are Sunnis. However, in Iraq, there are far fewer Sunnis than Shias. The Sunnis are close followers of the prophet, Mohammed. They believe that Mohammed was God's last, and most important, prophet on earth.

THE SHIAS: FOLLOWERS OF IMAM ALI

The word 'Shia' or 'Shiite' means 'a follower of Imam Ali'. Ali was the prophet Mohammed's cousin. After Mohammed died, Ali tried to lead the Muslim world. But most Muslims refused to accept him and the Shia group was formed. Imam Ali is buried in the city of Najaf.

Both Sunnis and Shias agree on one thing: the Koran is the word of God spoken through Mohammed. Both groups of believers follow its message closely.

What do you know about other world religions? Talk to a partner.

AND KURDS

THE KURDS: A PEOPLE WITHOUT A COUNTRY

The Kurds live in an area of mountains covering parts of Iraq, Turkey, Syria and Iran. They call it Kurdistan but it is not a country. They are the largest ethnic group in the world without their own country.

The history of Kurdistan is violent. For hundreds of years, their people have been persecuted by their neighbours. The worst attack happened in 1988 when Saddam's cousin, Ali Hasan al-Majid, destroyed around 1,200 Kurdish villages. During Saddam's rule around 300,000 Kurds were killed.

In the 1990s, things got better. The Kurdish area was protected by the USA and Britain, and called a 'safe haven'.

The safe haven meant that the Kurds were allowed to rule themselves. Later, after Saddam had gone, they held their own elections.

Today, most Kurds in Iraq realise that having their own country is not yet possible. They would like to see Iraq as a set of states, similar to the USA. Their state would be the largest. It would still be part of Iraq, but would manage the lives of its people on its own. Kurdish politicians would still be part of the government. Their dream of self-rule is also closer today than ever.

> **What do these words mean? You can use a dictionary.**
> **prophet**
> **bury   ethnic**
> **persecute   haven**

SELF-STUDY ACTIVITIES

INTRODUCTION–CHAPTER 1

Before you read
You can use a dictionary for this section.
1 Use these words to complete the sentences.
   **board   democracy   fragments   army   bombs
   occupy   checkpoint   soldier   bricks   abandon**
   a) People often play games on a … .
   b) Someone who carries a gun and wears a metal hat is a … .
   c) Many houses are made of … .
   d) A group of people who fight for their country in a war are an … .
   e) The idea of 'one person, one vote' exists in a … .
   f) A place where soldiers or policemen look at your papers before allowing you through is a … .
   g) When something like a glass breaks, the small pieces are called … .
   h) When an army attacks somewhere and stays there, they … that place.
   i) When someone leaves other people without any help, they … them.
   j) Soldiers often use … in wars. They make a very loud noise and can kill people and destroy buildings.

2 Look at 'People and Places' on pages 4–5 and answer the questions.
   a) Whose followers have their own newspaper?
   b) Who is a Shia leader in Naseriyah?
   c) Who lives with his grandmother?
   d) Who is Suleiman's father?
   e) Who thinks the US only attacked Iraq for its oil?
   f) In what city are the new Iraqi government's main offices?
   g) Where do people earn money from farming and making bricks?
   h) What is Iraq's fourth largest city?

After you read

3 Answer the questions.
   a) Why were the Sunnis fighting the Shias?
   b) Which group wanted their own state?
   c) Why did Mohammed stop going to school?
   d) Why didn't the Shias like Saddam Hussein?
   e) Is life less frightening for Mohammed after the war? Why?
   f) What three things did the Americans promise to the Iraqi people?
   g) Why does Mohammed have to fetch his boss's tea?

4 What do you think?
   'They only attacked us for the oil,' says Mohammed's boss about the Americans. Do you think he is right or wrong? Give reasons for your answer.

5 Writing
   Imagine you are an American soldier in Baghdad. Write a letter home to your family explaining how you feel and why.

CHAPTERS 2–3

Before you read

6 Complete the sentences with these words. You can use a dictionary.
   cheating   pray   security
   a) The streets of the city became very dangerous. There was no longer any … .
   b) 'That's not fair. You're … I'm not playing with you any more.'
   c) Religious people often get down on their knees and … to God.

7 At the end of Chapter 3, something changes in Mohammed's life. What do you think this change is?

SELF-STUDY ACTIVITIES

After you read

8 Are these sentences true or false?
   a) Mohammed wants to believe that his boss is a nice person.
   b) The boss never hits Mohammed.
   c) The boss is pleased that Saddam has gone.
   d) The boss wants Mohammed to go back to school.
   e) Mohammed is three years older than the rest of his class.
   f) Mohammed's father went to prison.
   g) The American soldiers kill a husband and wife.
   h) Mohammed can write his father's name.
   i) Mohammed finds a new job working in his uncle's garage.

9 Complete the sentences with the correct person.
   Mohammed   boss   neighbour   father   Saddam   teacher
   a) Mohammed's … helped him to write his name on the board.
   b) Mohammed's … was a policeman.
   c) After the Americans caught … they looked inside his mouth.
   d) … told his teacher he wanted to be a pilot.
   e) The …. shook Mohammed when he couldn't write his father's name.
   f) The … felt sorry for Mohammed and put an arm around his shoulder.

10 What do you think?
    Mohammed says to the boss that he prefers work to school. What does he really feel and why?

CHAPTERS 4–6

Before you read

11 Complete the sentences with these words. You can use a dictionary.
    **terrorist   chest   election   peaceful   tank   alcohol   power
    arrested   demonstration   torture**
    a) People vote for a new government in an … .

b) Selling or drinking ... is against Islamic law.
c) The ... was made of thick metal and had a huge gun on top.
d) They were unable to change the city's laws. They had no ... in local government.
e) There were thousands of people at the ... against the war.
f) The people wanted a ... life with no more fighting.
g) The police ... him for stealing the truck.
h) The ... took a bomb on the plane. He said he wanted to free his country.
i) The guards used ... to get information from their prisoners. They hurt them and didn't let them sleep.
j) The man was very strong. He brought the weight to his ... then lifted it up into the air.

After you read
12 Put these events in the right order.
   a) The Mehdi Army take the prisoners to a large house.
   b) The police arrest Mustapha Yacoubi.
   c) Sheikh Aws goes to a meeting about local elections.
   d) Twenty people are killed at the demonstration.
   e) The Mehdi Army free all the prisoners.
   f) Sheikh Aws tells his followers about the alcohol sellers at the market.
   g) The Shias go on a demonstration outside Najaf.
   h) The Mehdi Army go into the market.

13 What do you think?
   Moqtada al-Sadr and his followers don't believe that the Americans want to free Iraq. Why do they think this?

14 Writing
   Imagine you are a newspaper reporter. Write an account of the demonstration near Najaf on 4th April 2004.

SELF-STUDY ACTIVITIES

CHAPTERS 7–9

Before you read

15 Part Three is about the Kurds in the north of Iraq. Will the problems in this area be different from in Baghdad and the south of Iraq? Give reasons for your answer.

16 What do the words below mean? Write a sentence including each word. You can use a dictionary.
oven   wheat

After you read

17 Who said these things? Choose the correct person.
**Suleiman   Mahmoud   an old man   Bizhar   an Imam
a young girl   Bizhar's father**
a) 'We are like brothers.'
b) 'I want to go to college and get a good job.'
c) 'He destroyed our villages.'
d) 'I may not live to see the birth of a new Kurdistan. But I hope my children will see it.'
e) 'But this vote is more important than a hundred bombs.'
f) 'Our leaders have grown fat while our people go hungry.'
g) 'It will be hard for Kurds, Sunnis and Shias to live together.'
h) 'Iraq is not something you can cut into pieces.'

18 What do you think?
a) Will Suleiman be able to go to college in the end?
b) Why were the Kurdish people so excited about the elections?
c) Will Suleiman and Bizhar see the birth of a new Kurdistan?

CHAPTER 10 – EPILOGUE

Before you read
19 In Chapter 10 something changes in Suleiman's life. What do you think this change is?

After you read
20 Answer the questions.
   a) Why is Bizhar happy at the beginning of Chapter 10?
   b) Why is Suleiman sad?
   c) Why does Suleiman say he is lucky?
   d) Why did Baghdad become a little safer in 2007?
   e) What did Moqtada al-Sadr and his followers agree to do?
   g) What success have the Kurds had?
   h) When will American soldiers leave Iraq?
   i) What happened in November 2008?
   j) Which groups are fighting over Kirkuk?

21 Writing
   Imagine you are one of the people below. Write about your life in Iraq and your hopes for the future of your country.
   Mohammed   Mohammed's boss   Sheikh Aws   Suleiman

22 What do you think?
   a) *Iraq in Fragments* is a documentary film. Which parts of the film / story do you find the most interesting. Why?
   b) What do you think makes a good documentary film? List three things that you think are the most important.

GLOSSARY

Abu Ghraib
A city near Baghdad. It has a prison which was used by the Americans during the occupation.

Arab
An Arabic-speaking person from the Middle East or North Africa.

Baath Socialist Party
A political party. Saddam Hussein was its leader before his arrest.

Dawa Party
A Shia political party.

fundamentalist
A person who follows the rules of his or her religion exactly.

Hawza
A Shia religious training school.

Imam
An Islamic religious leader.

Imam Ali
The cousin of the prophet Mohammed.

Imam Hussein
The grandson of the prophet Mohammed.

Islam
The religion of Muslims.

Koran
The book of the Islamic religion.

Kurdistan
The homeland of the Kurds.

Kurds
A group of people who live in the north of Iraq. There are also Kurds in Turkey, Syria and Iran.

Mehdi Army
Moqtada al-Sadr's soldiers.

Middle East
A large area that includes countries such as Iraq, Saudi Arabia and Iran.

Mohammed
The messenger and prophet of God in Islam.

mosque
The special building where Muslims pray and listen to their Imam.

Muslim
A person who follows the religion of Islam.

Sheikh
An Arabic word that means 'elder'.

Shia
A Muslim who is a follower of the prophet Mohammed and Imam Ali.

Sunni
A Muslim who is a follower of the prophet Mohammed.

For more information on the film, go to:
www.iraqinfragments.com

IRAQ
IN FRAGMENTS